# DOOMED H

# ACCUSED OF WITCHCRAFT!

## Salem, 1692-1693

by Tim Cooke

**BEARPORT**
PUBLISHING

Minneapolis, Minnesota

Bearport Publishing Company Product Development Team
President: Jen Jenson; Director of Product Development: Spencer Brinker; Senior Editor: Allison Juda; Editor: Charly Haley; Associate Editor: Naomi Reich; Senior Designer: Colin O'Dea; Associate Designer: Elena Klinkner; Product Development Assistant: Anita Stasson

Brown Bear Books
Children's Publisher: Anne O'Daly; Design Manager: Keith Davis;
Picture Manager: Sophie Mortimer

Library of Congress Cataloging-in-Publication Data is available at www.loc.gov or upon request from the publisher.

ISBN: 979-8-88509-081-0 (hardcover)
ISBN: 979-8-88509-088-9 (paperback)
ISBN: 979-8-88509-095-7 (ebook)

For more information, write to Bearport Publishing, 5357 Penn Avenue South, Minneapolis, MN 55419. Printed in the United States of America.

# CONTENTS

A Puritanical World ...................... 4

The First Signs of Trouble ........... 6

Disaster Strikes ........................... 12

Life or Death ............................... 20

What Happened Next ................. 26

Key Dates ........................................... 30
Quiz ..................................................... 30
Glossary .............................................. 31
Index ................................................... 32
Read More .......................................... 32
Learn More Online ........................... 32

# A PURITANICAL WORLD

When two girls started acting strangely in a village in the **colony** of Massachusetts, people blamed evil **spirits**. Hundreds of people were accused of witchcraft, and 20 were killed.

Salem was home to English settlers who followed a strict form of Christianity called **Puritanism**. People of this religion believed the world was full of threats. Some of those threats included the physical dangers **Puritan** settlers faced after they arrived in the New World, such as **famine**, disease, and violent conflict with Native Americans. Puritans thought other threats came from an invisible world of evil spirits that worked for the devil.

# The Puritans

Witchcraft was a threat from the spirit world. Many Europeans believed in witches, and the Puritans brought that belief with them to New England. They thought witches sold their souls to **Satan** to gain special powers over their neighbors. From the 1300s to the late 1700s, people in Europe suspected of being witches were put on trial. Up to 60,000 people were **executed** for being witches.

In Europe, suspected witches were often burned to death.

# THE FIRST SIGNS OF TROUBLE

**Strange things started to happen at the home of Salem's pastor, Samuel Parris.**

Reverend Parris had arrived in Salem in 1689. His fiery **sermons** were popular with some villagers, including the powerful Putnam family. Other people thought he was only interested in how much money he could make. That made him unpopular in the nearby farming community that often struggled with hunger and **poverty**.

## A RICH NEIGHBOR

There were two Salems in New England. Just 10 miles (16 km) from the rural Puritan community of Salem Village was the bustling port of Salem Town. Salem Town was much richer than Salem Village. Villagers of Salem were jealous of their neighbors in town.

# Strange Happenings

One night, Reverend Parris's nine-year-old daughter, Betty, and eleven-year-old niece, Abigail Williams, began to twitch and shake uncontrollably. They twisted their bodies, screamed, and hid underneath their beds. After several nights, the girls' **symptoms** got worse. Parris asked Doctor William Gibbs to examine them. He decided the girls were "under an evil hand." He thought they were **bewitched** by the devil.

Abigail Williams lived with her uncle's family in Salem.

## Who's to Blame?

The girls in Samuel Parris's home were not the first people in New England to have similar **fits**. It had been happening for more than 20 years. Animals had suffered from fits, too, and some even died. Doctors could not explain symptoms such as temporary **paralysis** and blindness. Some Puritans began to whisper that the fits were the result of witchcraft.

## A SCIENTIFIC EXPLANATION

Scientists now think the girls' strange symptoms may have been caused by food. Puritan families ate bread made from rye. In the 1600s, rye contained a fungus called ergot. Ergot can cause visions, choking, and prickling of the skin. This may have been why people thought the girls were bewitched.

## Making a Cake

An enslaved woman named Tituba lived and worked in Reverend Parris's house. She practiced the **voodoo** religion. Parris told Tituba to make a cake to feed to the family dog. People believed dogs were witches' helpers. If the dog ate the cake, the spells on the girls would be broken. Then, the girls would be able to name the witches who had put them under a spell.

Tituba may have come to Massachusetts from the Caribbean island of Barbados.

The girls might have blamed Tituba because she was an enslaved person and therefore easy to pick on.

## Accused!

Everyone wanted to know who was causing Abigail and Betty's illness. The two girls blamed Tituba. They claimed they saw Tituba's evil spirit chasing them around the room. Then, their friend Ann Putman Jr. accused two other women in the village—Sarah Good and Sarah Osborne—of **possessing** the two girls.

# The Net Widens

Sarah Good had no home to live in and had once asked for food at the Parris house. She had been given nothing. Sarah Osborne was old and bed-ridden. She no longer went to church and had argued with the Putnam family. They were easy targets for accusations of witchcraft.

Puritans disapproved of people with little or no money like Sarah Good. They believed people should work to support themselves.

# DISASTER STRIKES

Accusations of witchcraft started to snowball. In just a few months, hundreds of people were accused and sent to trial.

The three women were put on trial in Salem. Sarah Good and Sarah Osborne denied being witches, but under pressure, Tituba eventually **confessed**. After long questioning by the **magistrates**, she described meeting Satan. She said he forced her to sign her name in his book. Tituba said the book also had the names of Sarah Good and Sarah Osborne.

## Sent to Jail

The three women were sent to jail in Boston, where they were questioned further. They were **shackled** in chains and kept in cells full of rats and lice. Like all prisoners at the time, the women had to pay for their filthy cells and terrible jail food. Meanwhile, panic was growing back in Salem.

# Witch Hunt!

In Salem, Betty and Abigail's fits continued. Soon, more girls started to claim they had been attacked by witches. There were reports of a shadowy beast that vanished into the air and of a large white dog that chased a man all the way home. Then, Ann Putnam Jr. accused three more people in the village of being witches.

## SPECTRAL EVIDENCE

In court, witnesses described being attacked by the spirits of the accused. Victims claimed that only they could see the attack. Puritans believed the devil could make witches invisible, so the courts accepted the victims' stories. This was known as spectral evidence.

# Arrested!

Ann said that Dorcas, Sarah Good's four-year-old daughter, had tried to force her to sign the devil's book. She also accused Martha Corey and Rebecca Nurse, two highly respected members of the church in Salem. Both women had disagreed with Reverend Parris when he had asked for a pay raise. Like Sarah Osborne, they had also argued with the Putnams. Dorcas and these two women were put on trial and sent to jail.

Puritans believed evil spirits could take many different shapes.

**The accusations the girls made about their neighbors were written down in careful detail.**

# A New Twist

By late April, another 15 women had been accused of witchcraft. They included Bridget Bishop, who lived in Salem Town and had never even been to Salem Village. Then, came a huge surprise. Ann Putnam Jr. and Abigail Williams accused a man named George Burroughs. Burroughs had been the pastor of Salem before Samuel Parris. He, too, was arrested and put in jail.

## Colony in Chaos

On May 14, 1692, the royal governor of Massachusetts, William Phips, returned to Boston after a long stay in England. He found the colony in chaos. The jails were full of people awaiting trial for being witches. There were new accusations all the time. It seemed that everyone was being accused!

Prisoners in jail were shackled by their wrists or ankles.

The chief judge was William Stoughton, lieutenant general of Massachusetts.

## A New Court

Phips immediately ordered a search to find judges for a special court in Boston to put the accused witches on trial. Seven judges were chosen. None had any experience with the law. Instead, they were wealthy merchants and landowners.

### PLEADING GUILTY

Accused witches could escape death if they admitted guilt. However, many of the defendants were strict Puritans. They believed God would punish them if they lied. They insisted they were **innocent**, even when it cost them their lives.

# The Trials Start

People wondered how the new court would decide who was guilty and who was innocent. A pastor from Boston named Samuel Willard argued that the devil worked in such sneaky ways that the judges had to use any means they could to rid Salem of its witches. That included taking spectral evidence seriously, as the earlier courts had done. The judges agreed.

The accusers often acted wildly during the trials.

# LIFE OR DEATH

The court decided whether accused witches were innocent or guilty. The guilty were sentenced to death.

The first person on trial was Bridget Bishop. She had many enemies who accused her of being a witch. She had been tried for witchcraft 12 years earlier but was found innocent. One man said the money she had paid him for work had disappeared from his pocket. Another claimed she had bewitched his son. One woman said Bridget's spirit had tried to drown her.

## A Sad End

A neighbor told the court how he had been attacked by a hairy monster with a man's face, a monkey's body, and a rooster's feet. The monster carried a message from the devil. When the man struck the monster with a stick, it flew out of the window. When he followed it outside, he saw Bridget walking by. The judges were convinced by this spectral evidence. They found Bridget guilty. On June 10, she was hanged.

Bridget's hanging took place at Gallows Hill, on the edge of Salem Town.

The accusers often had fits in court when they looked at the people they accused.

## More Trials

On June 29, the court met again for the trials of five more women. Witnesses told all kinds of strange stories about them. Sarah Good was found guilty and sentenced to death. Rebecca Nurse, a popular grandmother, was initially found not guilty. But her accusers complained so much in court that the judges decided to try her again. This time, they found her guilty.

## Not Just Women

The next trials included two men. George Burroughs was sentenced to hang. Just before he died, he prayed out loud. That shocked people, because witches were thought to be unable to pray. The elderly husband of Martha Corey, 80-year-old Giles Corey, refused to plead in court. He was sentenced to be squeezed to death beneath heavy stones.

George Burroughs shocked onlookers when he prayed on the gallows. That was not the behavior expected from a witch.

## IN THEIR OWN WORDS

Sarah Good told the official minister of the trials, Nicholas Noyes, "You are a lyer [liar] . . . I am no more a Witch than you are a Wizard; and if you take away my Life, God will give you Blood to drink." Rebecca Nurse declared, "The Lord knows I have not hurt them. I am an innocent person."

# The Tide Starts to Turn

The last eight victims of the witch hunt were hanged at Gallows Hill on September 22, 1692. They included Martha Corey and Ann Pudeator, who was found guilty of making a man fall out of a cherry tree. By now, however, people were starting to speak out against the executions. Mary Easty, the sister of Rebecca Nurse, was also condemned to death. She wrote a powerful **appeal** to the court to spare her and the others.

Martha Corey protests against her accusers in jail.

# MARY EASTY'S APPEAL

"I do not question that your honors work to the utmost of your Powers to uncover witchcraft and would not be guilty of Innocent blood for the world. But by my own Innocence, I know you are working in the wrong way."

Mary Easty wrote to the court to plead for her life and that of her sister, Rebecca.

## Second Thoughts

The accused witches filling the local jails included members of Salem's most respectable Puritan families. And, when not acting up in court, the girls who claimed to be victims of witchcraft seemed perfectly healthy and normal. People started to speak out against the trials.

# WHAT HAPPENED NEXT

As many of the accused were being hanged, more people started to question whether there could really be so many witches in Salem.

One of the first people to have doubts about the witch trials was Nathaniel Saltonstall, a judge at the court in Boston. He believed Bridget Bishop was innocent. He resigned from the court five days after Bridget was hanged. That same day, 14 church ministers from local towns sent the court a letter that questioned its actions.

The letter from the church ministers.

# End of the Trials

The letter was written by Cotton Mather, a respected Boston minister. It argued that the court should free suspects unless the judges were sure of their guilt. It also said spectral evidence should not be used. On October 6, the court released six suspects. Then, some powerful men, including Cotton Mather's father, Reverend Increase Mather, wrote another letter criticizing the witch trials. On October 29, Governor Phips stopped all further arrests. He shut down the court.

This house in Salem was home to Jonathan Corwin, one of the first judges to find the accused witches guilty.

## Changes Come

Things started to change in Salem. In 1694, Reverend Parris apologized for causing the witch hunt, but he was forced out of Salem by angry villagers. He was replaced as minister by Joseph Green, who worked hard to repair the damage done to Salem. In 1706, Green read his congregation Ann Putnam's apology for accusing innocent people of witchcraft.

# Proclaimed Innocent!

In 1711, Massachusetts overturned the guilty verdicts and paid money to the victims' families. A memorial to those who were executed was built in 1992. On Halloween 2001, almost 300 years after the trials and deaths, the last 11 people accused of witchcraft were finally declared innocent.

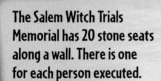

The Salem Witch Trials Memorial has 20 stone seats along a wall. There is one for each person executed.

## CHANGING THE LAWS

The Salem Witch Trials helped change the laws in America. The accused witches had no lawyers to help them and were seen as guilty from the start. After the trials, any accused person was thought to be innocent until proven guilty. Also, they were given the right to be represented and defended by a lawyer.

# KEY DATES

**1689** Samuel Parris becomes minister in Salem Village

**1692**

**January** Betty Parris and Abigail Williams start to have fits

**February 24** Dr Griggs declares them bewitched

**March 1** The first accused are questioned

**May 27** A special court is established in Boston

**June 10** Bridget Bishop is hanged for witchcraft

**July 19** Five women are hanged, including Sarah Good and Rebecca Nurse

**August 19** George Burroughs is one of five people to be hanged

**September 19** Giles Corey is pressed with heavy stones and dies two days later

**September 22** Ann Pudeator, Mary Easty, and others are hanged

**October 29** The special court is shut down

**1693** In May, everyone still in jail is freed

**1706** Ann Putnam apologizes for her part in the trials

**1992** The Salem Witch Trials Memorial is opened

**2001** Massachusetts officially declares all those convicted in 1692 innocent

## QUIZ

How much have you learned about the witch hunts in Salem? It's time to test your knowledge! Then, find the answers on page 32.

1. **Who were the Puritans?**
   a) Religious settlers in New England
   b) A local group of Native Americans
   c) Witches and wizards

2. **Who was the minister of Salem Village during the witch trials?**
   a) Reverend Burroughs
   b) Reverend Green
   c) Reverend Parris

3. **How were Betty and Abigail related?**
   a) They were not related
   b) They were cousins
   c) They were sisters

4. **How did the accused avoid being sentenced to death?**
   a) Plead innocent
   b) Say nothing
   c) Plead guilty

5. **When were the final victims declared innocent?**
   a) 2001
   b) 1711
   c) 1693

# GLOSSARY

**appeal** a request for a decision to be changed

**bewitched** under the control of someone else as a result of witchcraft or magic

**colony** a place or region that is ruled by another country

**confessed** admitted to committing a crime

**executed** killed as a type of legal punishment

**famine** a widespread shortage of food

**fits** sudden attacks of body movements that cannot be controlled

**innocent** not guilty of a crime or sin

**magistrates** government officials who can act as judges in court

**paralysis** a loss of the power to move or to feel part of the body

**pastor** a minister or religious leader of a church

**possessing** taking control of the mind and body of another person

**poverty** the state of being very poor

**Puritan** a member of a branch of the Protestant church in England and the New England colonies in the sixteenth and seventeenth centuries

**Puritanism** a strict form of Christianity

**Satan** another word for the devil

**sermons** speeches given during religious services

**shackled** bound and locked up in chains

**spectral evidence** stories of spirit-related events that are told by witnesses in court

**spirits** ghosts or supernatural beings

**symptoms** the physical signs of a disease or medical condition

**voodoo** a religious belief system found in some African and Caribbean cultures

# INDEX

**Bishop, Bridget** 16, 20, 26, 30

**Easty, Mary** 24–25, 30

**Good, Sarah** 10–12, 15, 22–23, 30

**Mather, Cotton** 26–27

**Nurse, Rebecca** 15, 22–24, 30

**Osborne, Sarah** 10–12, 15

**Parris family** 6–9, 11, 15–16, 28, 30

**Phips , William** 17–18, 27

**Puritans** 4–6, 8–9, 11, 14–15, 18, 25, 30

**Putnam, Ann** 10, 14–16, 28, 30

**Putnam family** 6, 11, 15

**spectral evidence** 14, 19, 21, 27

**spirits** 4, 10, 14–15, 20

**Tituba** 7–10, 12

**trials** 5, 12, 15, 18–20, 22–23, 25–27, 29–30

**witchcraft** 4–5, 8, 12, 16, 20, 25, 28–30

**witches** 5, 9, 11–12, 14, 17–20, 23–30

# READ MORE

**Burgan, Michael.** *The Salem Witch Trials: Mass Hysteria and Many Lives Lost (Tangled History)*. North Mankato, MN: Capstone Publishers, 2019.

**Light, Kate.** *Questions and Answers about the Salem Witch Trials (Eye on Historical Sources)*. New York: PowerKids Press, 2019.

**Loh-Hagan, Virginia.** *Salem Witch Trials (Surviving History)*. Ann Arbor, MI: Cherry Lake Publishing, 2021.

# LEARN MORE ONLINE

**1**. Go to **www.factsurfer.com** or scan the QR code below.

**2**. Enter **"Accused of Witchcraft"** into the search box.

**3**. Click on the cover of this book to see a list of websites.

Answers to the quiz on page 30

Answers: 1) A; 2) C; 3) B; 4) C; 5) A